The Business Of The Dancer

The Business Of The Dancer

Edward Case
Poems

KASEOWITZ
PUBLISHING

* * *

Publisher's Cataloging-in-Publication
Names: Case, Edward, 1923-1985, author. | Case, James, 1957- writer of
  supplementary textual content.
Title: The business of the dancer : poems / Edward Case ; [introduction and notes
  by James Case].
Description: First edition. | Township of Washington, NJ : Kaseowitz LLC, [2026]
Identifiers: LCCN: 2026901709 | ISBN: 9798994470800 (paperback) |
  9798994470817 (hardcover) | 9798994470824 (e-book)
Subjects: LCSH: Case, Edward, 1923-1985. | American poetry--20th century. |
  Philosophy--Poetry. | Life--Poetry. | Mortality--Poetry. | Politics and
  culture--United States--Poetry. | Love--Poetry. | Nature--Poetry. |
  Philosophy of nature--Poetry. | United States--Intellectual life--Poetry. |
  LCGFT: Poetry. | BISAC: POETRY / American / General.
Classification: LCC: PS3505.A8134 B87 2026 | DDC: 811/.54--dc23

* * *

Published in 2026 by
Kaseowitz Publishing
An imprint of Kaseowitz LLC
P.O. Box 74
Hillsdale, NJ 07642
United States of America

www.KaseowitzPublishing.com

* * *

Book design by James Case

Image credits:
Photograph of Edward Case, Cover, by Doris Case, 1949
Photograph of Edward Case, page xii, by Doris Case, 1955
Photograph of Edward Case, page xiv, by James Case, 1985

* * *

First printing 2026
Printed in the United States of America

* * *

Had Edward Case lived to see this book published,
this page would have likely read simply:

To Doris

*　*　*

A Note of Gratitude
By James Case

I am grateful to Hilton Kramer and Robert Richman—former
Editor and Poetry Editor, respectively, of *The New Criterion*—
who first published five of my father's poems shortly after his
death in 1985.

Likewise, I am grateful to Joseph Epstein, former editor of *The
American Scholar*, for first publishing two additional poems by
Edward Case, also posthumously, in 1985 and 1986.

As my father did not live to see his work published as a book, it
remains striking that a relatively unknown poet received such
posthumous recognition from periodicals of this stature.

Finally, I wish to thank Patrick Kurp, who in 2024 encountered
my father's poems in the periodicals mentioned above and wrote
about them in his widely respected literary blog, *Anecdotal
Evidence*. This led to our correspondence and, ultimately, to his
generous and invaluable encouragement, wisdom, and insight
as this book took shape.

*　*　*

ACKNOWLEDGEMENTS

Acknowledgement is made to the publications
in which the following poems first appeared:

In Memoriam: Ernst Cassirer
The Philosophy of Ernst Cassirer, edited by Paul Arthur Schilpp
The Library of Living Philosophers, Inc., Volume VI, 1949, p. 40

When We Heard The Old Philosopher (For W. P. Montague)
Saturday Review of Literature, Vol. XXXIII, No. 35, September 2, 1950, p. 12

They Have Fallen In Hate With Love
Saturday Review, January 19, 1952, p. 31

Great Workings Have No Sound (For a Statesman)
The Freeman, March 24, 1952, p. 408

Prophecy
The Freeman, July 28, 1952, p. 733

A Voluntary For Doctor Johnson
Modern Age, Volume 2, Number 3, Summer 1958, p. 311

Everything Is Possible To The Cheerful Hero
The New Criterion, Volume 4, Number 2, October 1985, p. 45

1914
The New Criterion, Volume 4, Number 2, October 1985, p. 46

A Victory Is Won
The New Criterion, Volume 4, Number 2, October 1985, p. 47

In a Brand New Buick Passing The Reputed Area Of My Grandfather's Grave
The New Criterion, Volume 4, Number 2, October 1985, p. 48

Minor Poet
The New Criterion, Volume 4, Number 2, October 1985, p. 48

As Grammarians
The American Scholar, Winter 1985/86, p. 43

The Business Of The Dancer
The American Scholar, Spring 1986, p. 226

* * *

CONTENTS

The Business Of The Dancer

CONTENTS

The Business Of The Dancer (cont.)

CONTENTS

* * *

Edward Case, 1955

INTRODUCTION

By James Case

THIS IS A COLLECTION of poems by a poet who died forty-one years ago. My father, Edward Case, was born on January 4, 1923, and died unexpectedly on July 10, 1985, at age 62 from a sudden illness. Shortly before his death, he assembled a collection of 75 poems from more than 150 he had written throughout his life. He hoped to publish them as a book titled *The Business Of The Dancer*, which is also the title of the collection's first poem.

My father arranged the poems in a loose-leaf binder divided into two sections, "The Business Of The Dancer" (55 poems) and "Additional Poems" (20 poems). After his death, I saved the binder along with his other poems and papers. For the next forty years, it sat on a shelf above my desk. Then I retired from my career as an architect to pursue long-delayed projects, including the publication of this book.

*　　*　　*

SOME OF THE POEMS in *The Business Of The Dancer* were previously published in *The New Criterion, The American Scholar, Modern Age, The Freeman, Saturday Review,* and in a book on the philosopher Ernst Cassirer (see Acknowledgments on page vii).

*　　*　　*

EDWARD CASE'S POETRY is formal, often employing rhyme and meter. The poems are efficient, with no excess. While accessible, they exhibit nuanced complexity, with words often bearing multiple meanings. The tone is philosophical, with observations on life, mortality, politics, love, nature, and the nature of things. Serious but not without wit, the poems are the work of a well-read, broad intellect.

*　　*　　*

MY FATHER GREW UP in the Bronx, New York City, the only child of Jewish parents. A major formative event in his early life occurred at age fifteen when, after completing ninth grade at what had just become the Bronx High School of Science, his right kidney was damaged, causing him to

Edward Case, 1985

miss tenth grade, spend a year in a hospital, and eventually have the kidney removed. A voracious reader, his love of books was reinforced by this experience, since there was little else to pass the time. At age sixteen, he was accepted into New York University where he earned a B.A. degree and then continued to Columbia University Graduate School of Philosophy. There, in a class on metaphysics, he met fellow student Doris Friedman, my future mother. They married in 1949.

In the 1950s, Edward Case was a book-review columnist for *The Wall Street Journal* and *National Review*. Through this, he forged relationships with many literary figures. Eventually, he founded a syndicated weekly literary journal titled *Classic Features* in which he published not only his own book reviews but also reviews and essays by other critics. Newspapers around the country subscribed to and published the literary criticism provided by *Classic Features*.

By the end of the 1950s, with a growing family, expenses exceeded what my father could earn from writing book reviews and columns. He therefore began to devote more time to business. From 1950 until his death, he was a shareholder in a small company that manufactured fluid-sealing products for industrial pumps, a business his father had started after World War I. Beginning in 1960, my father served as the company's president and CEO.

In 1963, my parents moved my three sisters and me from Manhattan to Weston, Connecticut. There, my father became involved in local politics and was elected to the Board of Education, serving as its chairman beginning in the late 1960s.

My father and mother enjoyed classical music and the New York City Ballet and held season tickets at the Metropolitan Opera. In later years, they enjoyed traveling overseas. It was during a trip to Italy that my father became fatally ill.

*   *   *

EDWARD CASE WAS a serious poet. He once said he found fulfillment in all his endeavors. Poetry was his artistic passion, but he also derived satisfaction from writing book reviews, from public service, and from business. Given that perspective, the title he chose for this collection of poems seems fitting.

*   *   *

The Business Of The Dancer

The Business Of The Dancer
(For Balanchine)

The business of the dancer
Measures life and death.
His body is a standard
Borne on his leaping breath.
Earth must not deceive him
Or he will trip and fall,
Nor must heaven grieve him
Who cannot grasp it all.
Between flux and order
He mediates a border.
Thus the dancing priest
Sanctifies the feast.

Mad At The Night

Slanging the dusk
A jazz blue jay
Flew at the dark
To squawk it away:
Mortality crying,
Not soft for the light,
Not scared of the dying
But mad at the night.

Blinding Truth

Blinding truth
Is the brother
    Of darkness.
We are formed
Unfit to see
The relative ends
    Of mystery.

For black hole
Or flaring sun
Our thread of vision
Is not spun,
But we are made
To net the fireflies
    Of the shade.

A Victory Is Won

When the fur-denned eye of the trancing bear
Stuck with fantastic honey opens and sees
The broken dark of shadowy tomorrow
And the first growl of life blows hunger through
The fatty air of feastless winter's dream
And the truth of claws and fleas and drool
And the scratch and hustle of the belly's urge
Lumber that monstrous sleeping bag to stretch
And shake the fearful bludgeoning paws
Deft enough to spear the silver salmon,
Tough enough to fend the bee-tree's bitter lance
And cruel enough to choke the pretty doe,
When such puissance uprises from such lumpen
Shamble, then a victory is won,
Not of the pure nor the ignoble,
But of that flesh which is the meat of stars,
That fist which flowers the bramble and milks
The sun.

As Grammarians

This life which is a sentence
Is also a declaration.
We make the sense of it
In our own terms.
As grammarians
We assert our meaning,
In what we decline,
In what we affirm,
In the conjugation of love,
In the predicates
And imperatives
And ambiguities
Of prosaic choice
We essay briefly
To define ourselves
Before the stop.

Time Is The Flame

Time is the flame
Tapering
The twining of our lives
In flickers
Of shadow and spark.
Together
We are the smoke
And flash
Of uncertain fire:
Wavering
By breath's grace
Till we expire
We light a space
Before the dark.

To Summerize The Thorn

To summerize the thorn
Is the essential point of rose.
Siren of sight and smell,
Efflorescent bell,
Luring the witless grasp
To seize the rooted asp:
The rose is summer's fool.
It is the sharp thorn's tool.

Willows Which Bind The Brink

Willows which bind the brink
Down deep are strong;
Who compromise with wind
To bank which else would sink
May keep
A separate bent.
The nod which recognizes
Need not be assent.

I Hear The Roll And The Raging Of The Drum

By yards the rulers tape their footless lines
To guile the mile-begetting inch for their
Measureless designs, while number men give
Keener minds to machines and seek endless
Answers by circuiting means. Everyman's
Castle is wiry with power. His eyes are beamed
To him through the tower. He's lashed to the wheel
He thinks he steers, great Lord of the button
But slave of the gears. Computers like tumors
Eat meat of his brain. He's ultimate tool
In a world without fix, where tinkers are boss,
Where Everyman's gain is any man's loss.
Beneath the trafficking hustle and hum
I hear the roll and the raging of the drum.

Venus Reserved

Venus
    from the foam
Emerges slowly,
Her motion
    languid
As the mooning
    ocean.
Not as a shore-bound
    swimmer
Does she rise,
At risk in an element
    of surprise,
But as one
Shaped of spume
And sun,
    at home,
Her fingers inlets
Of the fluent tide
Masking the shallows
Of that deep art
Which she
And the green sea
    hide.

Mercury

Mercury
Snapped in flight
Smiles vacuously,
Netted by calculus
Into a pinioned jake.
Approximate truth
Is a take
Which meanly lies:
Bear witness, his winged
And prisoned eyes.

The Motley Wise Man

In a world of fools
The motley wise man schools
Himself in simulation.
In salamander guise
He foils foolish eyes
To find a safer station.
If the world should shift
And wisdom then prove wise
He may unwrap his birthday gift
And need not sham surprise.
Till then, while clowns are kings
And jesters keep the keys,
Wisdom, in brays of folly,
Hides in asininities.

**Everything Is Possible
To The Cheerful Hero**

I shall piss against the North Wind
And make rain in Alaska.
I shall stamp my foot — *thus* —
And give migraine to all Manchuria.
I shall spit but once in the Mississippi
And swamp the souring cane of Cuba.
Even — *forbid it* — by bursitis disjointed
I shall beat out spanking rhythms
On every mono-buttocked bum
Who squats the seat of power.
I shall do more wonders to astound you!
I shall grow avocados in a concrete mixer
Whilst pouring foundations for plastic plants.
I shall explain life to you,
As well as electricity, gravity, money,
Magnetism and the reason for fireflies.
I shall make you glad you are yourself.

Truly, everything is possible to the cheerful hero
As nothing is improbable to the sober wise:
Palmy Eden awaits his outstretched hand
And he goes to Heaven when he dies.

Dallas Is A City Of Believers

Dallas is a City of Believers:
Worshippers of solid ground;
Diviners of flowing oil;
Adorers of blue sky
And scholasts of pinpoint landings;
Sacrificers to credit cards;
Preachers of freeways;
Proselytes of conditioned air
And heated unconditional truths;
Missioners of good works
With tall-storied offices;
Witnesses of television;
Circuit riders of electronics;
Converters of cotton;
Exegetes of balanced books;
Blessers of bourbon;
Cantors of slogans;
Readers of digesting tracts;
Theologues of golf and football;
Idolators of meat on hoof and grill;
Acolytes of short-haired men long in the saddle;
Sanctifiers of blondes and sports cars;
Creditors of cults and culture;
Scorners of the whys that blind.

Dallas is a City of Believers.
It is the oldest town on earth.
It is no place for prostrate grievers
To pray for New Jerusalem's birth.

A Voluntary For Doctor Johnson

Gentlemen, let us tie the tongue of talk
And be silent — bid the trumpeter sound
A voluntary for Doctor Johnson.

A voluntary for Doctor Johnson
Whose carcass gross as far-gone pregnancy
Concealed the fearful wonder of a child;
Who couched himself in the cushioned phrase
Of dogma and felt it creak against his weight
And pound of anguish;
Who cheered himself with the sound of voices
And tilted his tongue against his terror
And talked, talked, talked, till Despair herself despaired
And like a squelched woman bit her lip and schemed.

Gentlemen, let us tie the tongue of talk
And be silent — bid the trumpeter sound
A voluntary for Doctor Johnson.

A voluntary for Doctor Johnson
Who in his fright conversed against the night
And talked down speechless death.

As A Lover Might

Knowing that what I do not do now I shall
        always regret,
As a psalmist might who, hearing harmony
        in the night,
Scorned the dull task of penning and awoke
        to unrecall;
Knowing that what I do not do now I shall
        always regret,
As a surgeon might, postponing the unction of knives
To find lungless death the sick man's unaired
        cover-all;
Knowing that what I do not do now I shall
        always regret,
As a soldier might who, faltering in battle,
Had not the forward heart to stay his backward
        crawl;
Knowing that what I do not do now I shall
        always regret,
As a lover might, who does not ever tell his love
        at all.

When We Heard The Old Philosopher
(For W.P. Montague)

When we heard the old philosopher discourse
On great men known to him in youth,
And this so sweetly
      almost we believed
That the slow eddying dust in the mellowing
          sunbeams
Was the unstill dust of Athens, oh so lately fallen;
When we heard him who had witnessed
    skirmishes and winged encounters,
     high-flung engagements in lofty zones
        of light,
And when we saw in him peace and great candor,
And that like forest birds in deep afternoon
    his thoughts flashed upward,
        Then did we know
        What Plato had of Socrates,
        And what Spinoza knew
        When he heard the holy music
        Of high geometries.

The Burden Of The Hunchback

The burden of the hunchback
Is more than flesh and bone.
He's shaped into a question
He does not ask alone.
The query is no light one,
Dark weights of space and time
Depend upon the reason
And wait upon the rhyme.

The Pensive Dwarf

The measured thought
Of the pensive dwarf
Is immeasurably weary.
Lacking elegant form of proof,
Not big enough to stand aloof,
His problem of small dimension
Is limitless in extension.
The blankness of his disbelief
Has no logical relief:
His is a grief in theory.

The Man Who's In The Pit

The man who's in the pit
Should steal himself a bit
And chisel a bigger cell
And dig himself a well
And cut the rock with stairs
And sweat away his scares.
To carve a dream on stone
Makes him less alone.
Doing the best he can
By bits he is a man.

Second Rate

To be charged at second rate
By economizing fate
Is humbling to a sport
However much he's short.
Yet if he were asked more
And had not cash in store
What credit could he claim
To pay the tab of fame?

The charge of fate is fair.
If the rate is hard to bear
How much harder still
Not to fill the bill?

The Black Blind Man

In the subway
With cup and cane
The black blind man
Tapped a silver vein.

Some rang a coin
To see him by;
Others more softly
Bilked his eye.

To beggar darkness
Under ground or sky,
Some men delve,
Some men fly.

You Don't Have To Be So Smart

If you want a pound of wit
An epigram will fit.
Even an ounce of sense
Is weighty though not dense.
With minimal reflection
You may glass perfection.
A drop of thought's enough.
Wisdom is heavy stuff.

In Memoriam: Max Tobey

What is left, at the end, to sift
The incoherent dust
But the word, which is the memory
Of something in trust?

When even shadow's pith
Has withered half a plane
And icons of shadows crumble
Only words remain.

Thus, at final silence,
When nothing is seen or heard,
Eternity depends
On the power of the word.

In Memoriam: Ernst Cassirer

This is the locust season of our days
When the ripe meadows of the mind are bare,
This is the month of the never-born maize
Upon whose golden meats we shall not fare.
This is the week of the stunted stalk
And fruit that is dust on the bones of rock,
This is the day of the hungry hawk
And the songbirds dead by the fallen flock.
This is the noon of our derelict plain,
The sun-parched hour of most desolate pain.

Yet there is a valley where sweet grain grows
In strong-rooted stands, in tall splendid rows.
Here toiled in the meadows a man wise and serene,
And the meadows bore fruit and the meadows are green.

On The Death Of A Small Boy

Run through the gate, child.
Run, run,
            down to the garden
Where the brook flows
And the wind blows
And the laughing willows of repose
No longer weep.

Run through the gate, child.
Don't fear, don't fear.
Nothing here
            will harm you.
Run, run,
            down to the garden
Where the brook flows,
Where no thing evil ever goes
Where the tiger lily lies down
With the rose
In sleep.

To The Newborn

We must send ambassadors
        to the children
So that we may know them.
To the new nation
        in the forbidden land of time,
To the new empire
        colonized in the perilous night
We must send envoys
        for our vigilance.

Now, in love's trembling triremes
        oared by our unease
We must send courteous emissaries
        wise and soft in speech.

We must send ambassadors
        to the children,
    Now must we send them:
So that in the old age,
        in the white hairs
Of our long dominion
    We shall not curse the ecstasy
    Of our ancient exploration.

The Fury Of The Bee

The fury of the bee
Is his artistry.
Distraction makes him sting,
Order is his thing.
Discord makes him sour,
He likes the bedded flower.
Such is droning art
Without the honey part:
Sweet security,
The hive's Academy.

Lines For Smart And Clare

As an owl in a howling wood
In mad song my sanity abides.
In shadows where the creeper stalks
My lack-o-lantern reason hides.
What dangles from the weeping bough,
What lurks behind the barking tree,
What from the blackness screams for light,
All share the wilds with me.
Oh ye who dwell in Pleasance Park,
Hear with pity mine unkempt lay
And know how close the brush of dark
And how dense the other side of day.

Vial Thought

Death,
Sweet death,
Essential whale
And flower
Entombed in glass:
Sweet death:
Monstrous flesh,
Genitals of grass:
The mortal stink.

Like The Banished Burning Sumac

U n y i e l d i n g   t r u t h
Like the banished burning sumac
Must be bold.
Which in hostile fields
Takes root must hold,
Seize earth, stab sun,
Break rock and shade
The savage weed
Or fold.

U n y i e l d i n g   t r u t h
Like the banished burning sumac
Must be brave,
Common ground its fortress
Or its grave.

Only Grey Abstraction Serves

The man of sensitivity
Has extra sensuality.
His nose has teeth to bite the air;
His eyes have tongues to taste their stare;
His palate has eyes to scan his meal;
His ears palpably can feel;
His hand shakes with high frequency.

Yet, wary instrument, weary soul,
He cannot ever sense the whole.
To transcend apertures and nerves
Only grey abstraction serves.

Compromise

Compromise, two-faced, both-sided God,
Contemplating the half-loaves and the watered wine,
Is half-appalled and half-appeased,
Half-sorrowed and half-pleased.

Straddling the fence which is his sign
To the hemi-haunched who love him best,
He hears with demi-urgent zest
The half-measured glee by which he's blessed.
Mild the incense in his shrine.

"Come ye half in hope, half-blind,
Half of heart and half of mind....."

He hears the prayer which begs the question.
No commandment his but a suggestion.

Thus The Neutral Mind

In the valley it is still,
Silence is a hill.
Peace is such a place
Hollowed out of space.
The view is hemmed by height
Which limits wider sight
And turns the questing eye
Inward or to sky.
But Heaven, too, is small
When bounded by a wall,
And mountain views are bold
But mountain-tops are cold.
For most of us the plain
Is easier terrain.
Thus the neutral mind
Unclosed is self-confined.

A Balance To The World

Still, there's a balance to the world,
Impurity's the stuff of sense.
Heaven and hell are purer realms,
Earth being earthly and more dense
Thus catching light, since fact's opaque
And proving that the sun is there
And proving darkness is no fake
Validates time with years to spare.
Day is the brighter side of black,
The proof of gold confirms the lack.
Shadows are the darker side of light.
Day by day compels each night.

They Have Fallen In Hate
With Love

It is what they dream
On the hard cots of night
When rock-pillowed pride
Slaps truth's open face
And rough-blanketed rage
Is all that they embrace.

It is what they dream
In their loveless sleep
Who count tigers
As other men count sheep.
They have fallen in hate with love.
Merits they cannot claim
Nor respect demand:
They cannot command love
Hence they must command.

Top Banana

Like some mad old Comic
Whose audience has died
He has captivated me
To compel my applause.
To survive His clap-trap
I roar with laughter.
Then His joke and mine
Are joined thereafter.

The Promise Of Wings
(For Shcharansky And Sakharov)

Blessed are the birds of Russia
    In their flight.
The fettered eye which soars with them
    Though chained to a serf
Exercises freedom, strengthens sight
And by that practiced vision
Learns to brave the light.

Over a crouching land
    The promise of wings.
In a helmet-gray sky
    A bird
        Sings.

I Summon No Armies

I summon no armies to my banner.

My privacy is not rank enough.

They would not come
Who muster to a thick-skinned drum.

I blow no brazen bugle.

I have no marshal might.

Indeed, I have no banner,
No herd of truth for which to fight,
No holy dirt, no bloody shirt,
No damned rite.

I signal unflagging war
Only by my code of light.

Lines On My Fiftieth Birthday

The wishful breath grows wane
With waxing candle power
And the drip of fifty years
Turns sugar coating sour.
Though to feast the heart may burn
And the faltering guts may ache:
<u>To hell with the frosting</u>
<u>And thank God for the cake!</u>

In Tug Of War

In tug of war with world
My little dog strains,
And whining is his way
Of telling of his pains.
No power that he has
As strong as chains.

Perhaps pathetic as
His plaint of wrong
Is all our art
Of poetry and song.
Perhaps we are leashed men
Our lives long.

Better to be still
And silent in our years,
To be like things of steel
Whose voiceless muscles feel
But do not utter fears.

What Is There Of Merit?

What is there of merit but the quest?
Achievement is a vector of surprise.
Uncertain is the reading of our eyes.
The surest things we know are but surmise.
What is there of valor but the test
When the bravest answers may be lies?

Every Man Has His Scar

Every man has his scar and disfavor.
The beautiful people are not wholly so.
Then trust the crippled, daft and homely
But beware the fault you do not know.

Every man's face has a side that's better.
The ugly people are not wholly so.
Then trust the upright, wise and comely
But beware the good which does not show.

The Shade Of The Philosopher King
Meditates On Glory

"Only the bones of our greatness remain,
Inarticulate time whispering whitely
Of the insubstantial flesh, the lost heart,
The sod which was brain and gut, the fluid
Of vein and gland, the holy waters
Of life risen to rain and snow and ice
Fallen through ages to the green world or sea.

"The fossil slave outlasts our sculptured empire
And monumental bone resigns our majesty."

1914

The pearly throat of that peacock age was torn
In summer and its shriek yet grows, screaming
Unheard in all our days and deeds, like static
From a falling star, unseeming as the dust
Of space, yet crying murder as it bleeds.
So the voiceless moon imparting gravity
To frivolous tides roils the world unseen
But never hides its light nor ever slows.

Slain then the nightingale and the steed,
The garden wall then fallen, the enchanted
Wood a tiring room for weary death
And summer's lawn sown to widows' weed.
For winter came in August killing fruit and seed.
In that broken season forever died the rose.

Prophecy

When chicken-hawks scream
And hens don't cower,
That will be the year
The day and the hour.

When the fangs of snakes
Are milked for honey,
When greed has no stomach
And misers shun money,
When virus brings balm
To the bustling blood,
When the worm scorns man
And vomits on mud,
When love has no sorrow
And fools are not praised,
When the wage-scale of Sin
Is finally raised,
When atoms whirl slow
To the shepherd's flute,
When rockets won't fly
And cannon won't shoot.....

When chicken-hawks scream
And hens don't cower,
When tyrants grow weary
Of their power —
That will be the year
The day and the hour.

Business Cycle

Perhaps prudence could have prevented it.
Perhaps the cycle was in the structure.
Perhaps the spotted sun spewed crazy plague
When paralysis wasted economy
And through unrest and panic to final
Slump all industry was unrewarded,
Stock irrevocably deflated, bonds
Defaulted, all money unredeemable
For any goods, and no dividend was paid,
All thrift become thriftless, all savings unsaved,
All being lost in the minor depression
Where his coffin was laid.

Love Which Is More

Love which is more
Than flesh can bare
Garbs itself
In modest wear.
It habits in
A plainer fashion
The purer style
Of pantless passion.

But when unshifting
Truth is told
Warm skin is cloak
Enough for cold.

**To The South
In A Troubled Time**

Let the sons forget the fathers.
Let the fathers foresee the sons.
Let the clear brain
Be unpigmented by shades.
Let the rude host
Be civilly unacknowledged
And the private man
Esteemed out of uniform.
Let the heart not be a drum.
Let the eye not be invasion.
Let the teeth be clenched fortresses
Damning the throaty tide of war.
Let the flesh be no banner.
Let all men be of spirit
And unafraid of ghosts.
Let grey hate,
Fall-out of black and white,
Vanish now between
This morning and that night.

Watch The Kingly Critic Pass

With slang of symbol
And blare of brass,
Watch the kingly critic pass,
While the helot artist kneels
For royal crumbs
Which make his meals.

Where, alas, is the simple child,
Brave and brash and unbeguiled,
Who'll pierce the voluminous cloak of sham
And cry bare-ass and brazen ham?

But Somehow Crudely Hammered

My songs but somehow crudely hammered —
Not for me as an etcher
    With blades.
My songs but somehow crudely hammered —
As a worker with stones,
As one who trades
Blows with steel-spined rock
Or pours the cauldroned lead
Or smashes the angry burning bars
Till anger is dead.

Villa-Lobos:
Bachianas Brasileiras

Black orchids fleshing
The grave and settled bones
Of a most exact and perfect prophet,
Ordering him
In a dark and passionate habit.....
The red parrots of sunset
Screaming at mountains.....
And the jaguar hours in the midnights
Of the mind's self-stalking.....
Rain forests of love
Bursting the continent heart.....
And the long current of life
Spitting its muddy course
To the slack mouth of dissolution.....
The heroic butterfly,
Frail and brave as rainbows.....
The voiceless woe
Of the sharp-tongued snake
Writhing ceaseless coils
Of an evil knowing.....
The subtle syllogism of ferns
Whispering eternal reasons
To the formless bogs.....
These, all these, are the music
Of Villa-Lobos,
Glaciers of flame, fire crystalline as snow.

Bearded Bards

Bearded bards keen of death.
Bald ones chant of life.
He keens less who kens the more
The keenness of the knife.

A Man With A Polytetrafluoroethylene* Soul

When a man with a polytetrafluoroethylene soul,
Pure white and impervious to passionate corrosion,
Finally wears out through mechanical erosion,
It would be most unwise
To subject him to cremation
For the unpleasant reason
That at five hundred fifty degrees of heat
His soul will sinter from his meat
And then poison you out of hand, lung and season.

Without acid sermon from the base
Who soil the cerements of grace,
Bury unassailable worth
Cryptically in neutral earth.

*The chemical name for a substance known by the DuPont
trade name Teflon

Minor Poet

Saved by a line
Before he sank
    Into the nameless sea:
His sentence stayed,
His passage paid
    Home free.

Additional Poems

By Black Perceptions Blind

The lights do not fail
      suddenly.
They fade
      until
Shadow
      becomes the eye's
         expectant see
And sun
      a cosmic fallacy.
Like the troglodyte
      we pale
         imperceptibly
By black perceptions
      blind,
To casual ignorance of fire
And common darkness
      of the mind.

Hassidim

To be closer
They keep their distance.
As shadows defining light
They wear black space formally,
Like the discreet livery
Of proud servants:
Black hats, the plane width of distance
And black coats the hiding lengths
In which they stoop.
They stare inward
Like blind astronomers.
Beneath the effacing beards
Countenance is immaterial.
Hair, pious, templed,
Argues intricately
For the guarded head
Covered against the glittering, temporal,
Perilous dust.
Beauty, which is of things, is dark.
The fire which sustains the world
Hides in a spark.

Lines On The Venetian Ghetto

Over the quiet, emptied square
Where the footfall of time is shod
In Florentine leather worn on the feet
Of the awful tourists of God
In ceaseless cabalistic line
The gulls ascend, incline,
Suggesting an abstract design.
The vigil of wings
Is — perhaps — a sign.

Written on the train from Venice to Rome, 10/19/82

To My Wife On Reaching
A Certain Age

Your years are but a string of beads
Tossed aside when we embrace,
Costume jewelry of common sort,
Silly beads of no import
Casually worn to take the place
Of sparkling treasures
You hide and grace.

My love is unadorned. It heeds
No distraction of worthless beads.

For Doris

This impermanent caress
Cannot smooth the world's distress
Nor soft hard truth with tenderness
That sures.

Yet, this impermanent caress
Lifting hand against the world's duress
And icy age's endlessness,
Endures.

Lines On My
Sixtieth Birthday

It is late.
Nothing will wait.
The stars in haste
Recede
And all things, great
And small, now speed
To ending.

Have I art
To seed the waste
Of yieldless time?
Have I heart
And reason,
Fruitful hope
And will transcending
My dying season?

In A Brand New Buick
Passing The Reputed Area
Of My Grandfather's Grave

My grandfather oscillant in a grave
Neither he nor I have seen,
Rocked, perhaps, by what I am
And what he might have been
Had he been the son of his son
And not my father's sire,
To what ease of body, cease of toil
He might then aspire,
Taking at first my common lot
Of property and possession
As miracle and bounty of the Lord
Blessing his succession,
Yet would he not, at six feet seventy years
And millennial mind's remove,
Seeing my yieldless discontent,
Tear his cerements, reprove
And mourn me dead as he below,
I having but exchanged his God for goods
And traded woe for woe?

Which Way You Jump

Which way you chance to jump
When you turn the garden path
And you come upon the tiger
Dozing in his wrath
      Is not innate.

Do not blame constricting genes
If you leap into the trap.
It is the chancy tiger
Awakened from his nap
      Whose jump is fate.

In The Second Sleep

In the second sleep
        of night
When the feeble ambition
Of the sun-struck moon
Is cast over,
Cold
        like a thought
        from the north
Falls
        to quiet
        cricketing dreams.
The senseless world
        seems
To center
        to a core
Where darkness
        is no more
        than light.

On The Portrait Of Miss Elizabeth Buckler
By Sir William Beechey—Hanging In
The Carnegie Institute In Pittsburgh

In the steel king's palace,
    his penance,
By one dimension lost
In infinite enchantment
She is forever
In her garden, a child
    with flowers in her hand.

In what hard mill
    is fragile beauty cast?
By what alloyed bars
    is she held fast?
What is her crime?

She does not know.
She is a dead king's thrall
Forever seized in tribute
    and atonement.

In that sterile hall,
Cold-lit, in the never-all-
    unfouled air,
Amidst numb and sightless
Scrawl-blinded throngs,
She smiles, Victress over rust and time
In the steel king's thongs.

Heraclitus On The Saugatuck

I am he
> who in a dark glance
>> saw the world
>>> burn blackly.
From the jet stream
> of incoherent youth
>> I cupped
>>> a muddy simile.

Now my humors are dry.

My lips crack a parchment smile.

In ultimate drought
I see the bottom of the spill.
Under the chattering waters
The bed of rock is still.

God Be Thanked For Illumination

God be thanked for illumination
Which brightens the labor of the eye.
Not for the mighty sun
Or the void-whelmed stars
Or the moon-struck sky,
But for that private magnitude of light
Which braves within and out
The blinding night.

Tula

Ultimately Thule is not so strange
    Or far.
We need no guidance
    From a star
To journey there.
Stones unsettled are not rare.

In that dismembered rocky heap
Is hardly a revelation.
In that eagle-eyed, harsh-lunged
    Thin-nostrilled air
Unremembered in the mindless
    Mountains' stare
What we see
    Is common share,
No farther than any common place
Which we, too, keep,
For a space.

November 17, 1983, Casa Sierra Nevada
San Miguel de Allende, Mexico

Follett's Garden

Follett's green memory springs from the grave
Recollecting the dissipate seed,
Swelling impotent winter's shrunken root,
Recalling the leaf and the bud and the shoot;
Oh Follett, from earthly chores ascended
What eternal memorial is yours
Which time by sun and rain restores unended
And the nurturing soil newly assures.

To Doris From Edward
June 26, 1974

When cedars were songs that night
And the wandering fingers of the shore
Stroked the trembling curve of the sea
And we were apart no more,
When a lonely piano cried
Night-music of wave and foam,
And enormous the moon was grown
And we were then alone
— On an island we two were
And ocean-long from home —
Then we made a melody
Of woods, winds and the fertile sea,
Under the moon I sang my song to you
and you sang, too, oh you sang, too,
For me.

1949

The Poet Contemplating
His Wrinkled Muse

Age, thou subtile plague
Poxing the fleshy sinner
As well the bony saint,
A venereal complaint
Which in the virgin womb doth rage,
Which waxes all the stronger
In him who strives the longer,
'Gainst which no muscled arm can fend,
Whose wound no chemistry can mend,
Greyer, grumbler, bumbler, gagger,
Palterer, fumbler, mumbler, sagger,
Falterer, stumbler, humbler, slayer:
I'll escape thee yet, in time,
And live ever in my rhyme.

I Write For That Youth

I write for that youth by an inward sea
Alone by the surf of his privacy
Which none could hear but he.
Not for worn-out dams, nor birth-bound girls,
Not for shorn old rams tethered by hornless age
Is my pity or my rage,
Nor for land-locked churls who hear no waves
And taste their salt as the sweat of slaves:
No, I write for him who heard the surge
But did not sense the tide diverge
And did not know that sun would burn his light
And darkness drench his torch of night
And the earth in the breaking sky turn round
And his world wash out without a sound.

Now I Have Died A Little

Now I have died a little.
I am a little old.
Though not for coffin ready,
Nor stone-weighed cold.
Now I have died a little,
And my dying is this:
What I cannot do, I see,
And what I shall miss.

My Bones Are Immortal

My bones are immortal.
They cannot die.
They are the cliffs
And the coral
Of me.
When my red seas perish
In final sand,
When unchosen life passes
To an unpromised land,
<u>My</u> <u>bones</u>
<u>Will</u> <u>be</u>.

My bones are immortal.
They cannot die.
By my bones
My words must lie,
Clean and white,
Lean and bright:
<u>Articulate</u>
<u>With</u> <u>light</u>.

Great Workings Have No Sound
(For A Statesman)

True constructions are quiet things
And great workings have no sound.
When the sun rises the strutting cock crows
And thinks, as he shrieks, that so the sun goes.
But no one hears the oak as it grows,
Or the air which feeds us, until it blows.

Music is after silent doing.
It is the done.
Noise is failure.
As the clash of gears in ill machines
Or good ends clashing with foulest means.

True constructions are quiet things
And great workings have no sound.
Beware of clamor and the cocks of fame,
Be unbribed by the cash of praise
And be undismayed by the duns of blame.
Make no noise, build silently in your high realm
Higher than the weak-lunged horizon of your time,
Build higher than the restraining rail of breath
Where airless, no noise is
And unsounds death.

NOTES

The following notes, prepared by the poet's son, James Case,
provide background on several of the poems.

The Black Blind Man
page 24

I BELIEVE THIS POEM was inspired by a blind man soliciting contributions for a local guild serving the blind, whom I remember seeing in the early 1960s when I was a small boy and would occasionally accompany my father on his commute. My father often encountered him during the morning rush hour on the Lexington Avenue subway platform under Union Square in Manhattan. He would always put money in the man's tin cup and exchange friendly banter with him—the blind man invariably in good humor. On one occasion, when I was six years old, I asked my father how this man could be so cheerful given his condition. My father, in a serious tone, said we should admire this blind man because, despite his affliction and the many opportunities denied him that I took for granted, he did not "delve" into self-pity but instead got up every morning and did what he was able, as every person should do, engaging the world with purpose, positivity, and persistence—his cheerfulness a testament to his strong character, fortitude, and resilience, attributes we should all strive for. Heavy stuff for a six-year-old, and an early lesson I still often reflect on.

In Memoriam: Max Tobey
page 26

DR. MAX TOBEY was a general practitioner and our family doctor. He was one of my father's dearest friends. Tobey was old-school—a strong, street-smart, principled, forthright, and generous man whose word was his bond. Raised in poverty in Manhattan's tough Hell's Kitchen neighborhood, Tobey managed to gain an education through athletic scholarships, eventually graduating from medical school in 1935. My father and Tobey first met in 1938, when my father, then age fifteen, fell ill and spent a year in a hospital, where he ultimately had a kidney removed. Tobey, then a young physician there, befriended him. My father and Tobey remained close friends for the rest of their lives, to the point that my sisters and I always referred to him as "Uncle Tobey," and his wife as "Aunt Edna." He was funny and warm, and we loved him like a real uncle.

In Memoriam: Ernst Cassirer

page 27

ERNST CASSIRER, the philosopher and scholar, was born in Breslau, Germany (later incorporated into Poland after the Second World War and renamed Wrocław) in 1874 and died an exiled Jew in New York City on July 28, 1945. He was an esteemed and beloved professor of philosophy at Columbia University when my father was a graduate student there. The volume *The Philosophy of Ernst Cassirer* was published posthumously in 1949. In it, the editor included my father's poem, *In Memoriam: Ernst Cassirer,* and the transcript of an address my father delivered at memorial services held for Cassirer at Columbia in 1945. My father's address was titled "A Student's Nachruf [obituary]," in which he spoke on behalf of the students regarding Cassirer's passing. The concluding paragraph of his address reads:

> And so we, the students of philosophy at Columbia, esteem it to have been a great privilege and a great honor in our lives that, in this great university of the New World, we were the last students of the lineal descendant of Immanuel Kant, that we were the last students of the last flowering of German philosophy. And I do not speak from paper or from notes or in words formulated coldly and with deliberation, but I speak from the heart when I say: *We loved Ernst Cassirer.**

**The Philosophy of Ernst Cassirer*, edited by Paul Arthur Schilpp, The Library of Living Philosophers, Inc., Volume VI, 1949.

A Man With A Polytetrafluoroethylene Soul

page 56

AS NOTED below this poem on page 56, polytetrafluoroethylene is a DuPont product commonly known by its trade name Teflon. From 1960 until his death in 1985, Edward Case supported his family as owner and CEO of a small industrial-products manufacturing company founded by his father that produced fluid-sealing products used in pumps (chemical pumps, food processing pumps, etc.). Teflon was a raw material used in the composition of some of their products. His company held many patents on products designed by their in-house engineer. At least ten patents, however, were for products designed by my father himself. Although his education and passions focused on literature and philosophy, he possessed a seemingly innate mathematical ability and was able to rapidly solve complex equations in his head, which gave him an advantage in business, including understanding the mechanics of fluid-sealing products. He attributed his mathematical ability to how math was taught in the excellent New York City public schools he attended in the 1930s, with their emphasis on rote memorization.

To My Wife On Reaching A Certain Age
For Doris
To Doris From Edward - June 26, 1974
Pages 64, 65, 75

MY FATHER met my mother, Doris Friedman (1923–2016), in the 1940s when they were graduate students in the philosophy program at Columbia University. They married on June 26, 1949; their marriage continued until my father's death in 1985.

In A Brand New Buick Passing The Reputed Area
Of My Grandfather's Grave
page 67

EDWARD CASE'S paternal grandfather was a young, impoverished, Orthodox rabbi who immigrated to the United States circa 1890 from Eastern Europe to escape persecution, settling in the tenements of Manhattan's densely populated Lower East Side. He never learned English, communicating only in Yiddish. Edward's childhood recollection of his grandfather was that he was a solemn, somewhat distant, bearded religious man with whom he had limited interaction. The Case family's journey of assimilation began with this poor immigrant rabbi, then passed to the rabbi's son (Edward's father)—born in the Lower East Side in 1896—who became a Modern Orthodox Jew, a United States Army veteran of the First World War, and a self-made businessman, and then to Edward—a not particularly observant Reform Jew, college-educated, intellectual, writer, poet, and businessman of upper-middle-class means living in the affluent New York City suburbs.

In 1964, my father and mother, Edward and Doris, built a home on five acres of wooded land along the east bank of the Saugatuck River in Weston, Connecticut, where they lived until Edward's death in 1985. There was a winding path from the house through the dense woods that led to a small wooden dock on the riverbank, twenty yards upstream from a loose stone dam through which the river flowed. Sometimes, on a hot summer afternoon, my father would swim to the dam and spend several hours repeatedly submerging himself under the water to the bottom, lifting large stones, one at a time, that had shifted or tumbled from the dam onto the riverbed, and replacing them on the dam. It was a solitary activity, in a secluded river surrounded by woods, affording a sort of therapeutic, meditative relaxation—a place to think, totally disconnected from the world. His poem *Heraclitus On The Saugatuck* was undoubtedly one result of his reflections during these escapes.

Follett's Garden

page 74

William Follett lived with his wife, Evelyn, on a twenty-acre property about a half mile north of our home on Valley Forge Road in Weston, Connecticut. For many years, the Folletts owned and operated a nursery there, growing and selling trees, bushes, and perennials. When our family moved to the area in 1964, Follett had already been retired for a few years and the nursery was shut down, but he still maintained a large flower and vegetable garden directly behind a low New England stone wall along the road. Born in England in 1890, Follett came to America in 1913 at age twenty-three but returned to England to join the British Army in the First World War. He fought in the Battle of Loos and was wounded at Mametz Wood during the ferocious Somme offensive. He returned to the U.S. in 1920, purchased the property on Valley Forge Road in 1927, and established his nursery business.

Occasionally on weekends, my father, while walking our dog, would stop along the way and chat for a few minutes with Follett, who was daily outside tending his roadside garden. Follett gave me the impression of being the quintessential Connecticut Yankee—in his overalls and straw hat, his knowledge of horticulture, his reserved demeanor, lean and fit, clearly a believer in good walls, and his civic-minded attitude (involved in his church, a former member of the town's school board, and a member of other civic organizations). The two men shared an affinity. Follett enjoyed my father's intellect, curiosity, humor, and far-reaching book smarts, and my father appreciated Follett's practical knowledge, Yankee independent spirit of self-reliance, historical perspective, and common sense.

Follett died in 1976, after which his garden went unattended and, over time, lost its clarity and regimented layout, returning each year in a progressively unkempt, overgrown state. The poem *Follett's Garden* is about this but also, clearly, a tribute to Follett himself—a good man, in my father's view, worthy of respect, who led a productive, principled life.

*　*　*

DATES

List of poems annotated with dates they were written:

CAPITALIZATION NOTE

Each word in the title of this book and in the titles of the poems begins with an uppercase letter. The titles do not follow the conventional practice of lowercasing short prepositions (of, in, to, for, etc.). This capitalization reflects how Edward Case originally typed these titles and is preserved here as an intentional stylistic choice, lending them a more formal, declarative presence consistent with Case's original mid-twentieth-century typescripts.

* * *

ABOUT THE TYPE

THE POEMS IN this book were originally typed by Edward Case using an ordinary mechanical typewriter, his preferred and primary tool for writing in both his literary and business work. He made very few handwritten drafts. Forty years after his death, his original typed sheets were scanned to create a PDF, which was then electronically converted for use in a publishing program and digitally arranged for this volume.

The initial design concept was to set this entire book in a typewriter-style typeface, such as Courier Prime or American Typewriter, as a stylistic gesture recalling Case's original typed sheets. Case, however, used a typewriter because, in his time, he did not have access to a personal computer with its range of fonts and graphic tools. His use of the typewriter was therefore a choice dictated by available technology and expedience, not aesthetics. This view is supported by the fact that on several occasions he had one or two poems printed on archival paper, set in a more classical serif typeface by a graphic artist, and framed as gifts. Accordingly, instead of a typewriter-style typeface, a more readable typeface and one better suited to the content and style of his poetry was selected for this book.

Poetry collections, especially those written in a more traditional or formalist mode, are often set in Garamond, Palatino, Baskerville, Bembo, and similar classical serif typefaces. Such faces enhance readability and render words more readily recognizable. The body of this book is set in Baskerville, named for its creator, John Baskerville, who developed the typeface in eighteenth-century England. An enduring neoclassical serif, it remains widely used today for its clarity, balance, and precision. Its crisp yet restrained character lends particular distinction to formal verse, allowing the structure and rhythm of the language to emerge with clarity. It is therefore well suited to this work by a formalist mid-twentieth-century poet and businessman. The titles on the front cover and title page, however, are set in Courier Prime, and the poem *As Grammarians* on the back cover is set in American Typewriter as gestures to the poems' original typed form.

* * *

www.ingramcontent.com/pod-product-compliance
Lightning Source LLC
Chambersburg PA
CBHW051442140726
47987CB00006B/2493